Novena to the Holy Spirit

Powerful Prayers to the Holy Spirit with Bible Reflections and Meditations

(Come Holy Spirit Prayer)

Table of Contents

FOREWORD

It was St. John Vianney, the Cure of Ars, who always say: "Without the Holy Spirit, all is cold. Therefore, when we feel we are losing our fervor, we must instantly start a novena to the Holy Spirit to pray for increase in faith and love."

The nine days after Christ went back to Heaven after his resurrection were spent in prayers and Meditations by our blessed mother Mary and the Apostles in preparation for the coming and outpouring of the Holy spirit This could be regarded as the first novena ever made in the Catholic Church. .it is a novena made at the Lord Command "Tarry here in Jerusalem until you are endued with the power of the Holy Spirit "(Luke 24:49). this novena to the Holy Spirit is the model for all other novenas and should hold a special place in our devotions.

We recall that St. Alphonsus said in his writings that: "The novena to the Holy Spirit is the mother of all novenas, because it was the first that was ever celebrated, and by the holy Mother of God with the Apostles in the Upper-room. And it is a novena prayer that was answered with many wonders and Gifts, majorly by the descent of the Holy Spirit,

Pope Leo XIII also advocates that a novena be made before the Feast of Pentecost in all parish churches to implore the return of heretics and schismatics to the True Faith.

These words from the scripture "The grace of the Lord Jesus Christ, the love of God, and the communion of the Holy Spirit be with all of you." **(2 Cor 13:13)** is a great indicator that the Holy Trinity makes us a part of their life! Catholic Catechism teaches that the mystery of the Holy Trinity is the "the central mystery of Christian faith and life" (#234).   The Holy Spirit is the spirit of love which found between the Father and the Son: it is eternal, totally self-giving in nature and pure. What better way would have God demonstrated his love for other than gifting us with his only son and to die for us in order that we may have eternal life?

As Catholics we received and are sealed with the Holy Spirit in the sacrament of confirmation. And at mass during consecration, the priest invokes the Holy Spirit to transubstantiate the bread and wine. Each occasion when we make the sign of the cross. We are invoking the holy Spirit

If you take a closer study of the scriptures, you will discover that the Spirit is seen everywhere in the bible especially in the New Testament. The Holy Spirit is far more than the symbols mentioned in scripture such as fire, wind, water, breath. The Holy Spirit is a person, a Someone, to whom scripture says that we can reach out to, he prays in us and his presence in our lives brings a lot of positive transformations in our lives.

The Holy Spirit makes us alive to the awesomeness of just being in God's presence. We get to that level of spirituality where God's presence becomes the most important priority in our lives. The Holy Spirit draws us into a deeper divine live with God, bring inward transformation and order our steps in all thing including our day to day choices in life and empowers us to be great witnesses for Christ

May he who is called The Gift of Gifts, the Sanctifier, the Interior Master, the Finger of God, Paraclete, Sweet Guest of the soul, the bond of love between Father and Son, Consoler and Counselor, the Soul-life giving principle of the Church, the Light from on high dwell richly in our heart with his seven gifts and twelve Fruits Amen .

Rev. Fr. Edward Broom, (O.S.S.)

Novena Intentions

- ✝ **For the Church and the Holy Father, the Pope**
- ✝ **For Spiritual Growth**
- ✝ **For healing of the sick**
- ✝ **For conversion of sinners**
- ✝ **For the dying and souls in Purgatory**
- ✝ **For Sins against the Holy Spirit.**

a. **Despair**

b. **Presumption**

c. **Impenitence**

d. **Obstinacy**

e. **Resisting Truth**

and   your Personal intentions.

Novena to the Holy Spirit

In the name of the Father and of the Son and of the Holy Spirit. Amen

Song:

Spirit of the living God, fall afresh on me.

Spirit of the living God, fall afresh on me.

Melt me, mold me, fill me, use me,

Spirit of the living God, fall afresh on me.

Spirit of the living God, fall afresh on us.

Spirit of the living God, fall afresh on us.

Melt us, mold us, fill us, use us,

Spirit of the living God, fall afresh on us

1 believe in God....

Our Father

Hail Mary

Glory Be

Act of Contrition
O my God, I am sorry I sinned against you, because you are so good, and by the help of your Grace I will not sin again. Amen.

Prayer To The Holy Spirit
Come, Holy Spirit, endue my heart with your Holy Gift, the Gift of love. Give me the gift of discernment. that i may see your acts in me

and all around me. Sanctify my ears that i may hear you amid the noisy world and in the lives of others. Use my hands to carry out the works of love without pre meditations. take my feet and carry me in faith and knowledge. Envelope my soul with the gift of light, that it may shine with love eternal. Amen.

O God, who instructed the hearts of the faithful by the light of the Holy Spirit, grant us in the same spirit to be truly wise and ever to rejoice in his consolation through Jesus Christ, our Lord. Amen.

Chaplet of the Holy Spirit

First Mystery: By the Holy Spirit is Jesus conceived of the Blessed Virgin Mary.

The Meditation: The Holy Ghost shall come upon thee, and the power of the highest shall overshadow you; therefore, the child to be born[h] will be called holy, the Son of God.

The Practice: Diligently implore the aid of the divine spirit to imitate the virtues of Jesus Christ, who is the model of virtues, so that you may conform to the image of the son of God.

Our Father

On the Small Beads: **Come Oh Holy Spirit and fill the heart of the faithful**....

Responds And enkindle in us the fire of your love. **(10 times)**

Send forth your Spirit and they shall be created,

And you shall renew the face of the earth.

Second Mystery: The Holy Spirit descended upon Jesus when he was baptized.

The Meditation: As soon as Jesus was baptized, he went up out of the water. At that moment heaven was opened, and he saw the Spirit of God descending like a dove and alighting on him (Mathew 3:16)

The Practice: Hold in highest esteem the priceless gift of sanctifying grace, infused into your soul by the Holy Spirit when you were baptized. Be faithful to your baptismal promises. Strive to grow always in, faith, hope and charity. Live always in a manner befitting a child of God and a member of his true church m so that you may obtain hereafter the inheritance of heaven

Our Father

On the Small Beads: **Come Oh Holy Spirit and fill the heart of the faithful**....

Responds And enkindle in us the fire of your love. **(10 times)**

Send forth your Spirit and they shall be created,

And you shall renew the face of the earth.

Third Mystery: Jesus was led into the wilderness by the Spirit in order to be tempted by the devil.

The Meditation: Jesus, full of the Holy Spirit, returned from the Jordan and was led by the Spirit in the wilderness, where for forty days he was tempted by the devil. He ate nothing at all during those days, and when they were over, he was famished (Luke 4:1- 2)

The Practice: Be ever grateful for the sevenfold gifts of the holy Spirit bestowed upon you in confirmation., for the spirit of wisdom and understanding, of counsel and fortitude, of knowledge and piety, and of the fear of the Lord . be guided by him always, so that in all the truth and temptations of this life you may act as a true Christian.

Our Father

On the Small Beads: **Come Oh Holy Spirit and fill the heart of the faithful**....

Responds And enkindle in us the fire of your love. **(10 times)**

Send forth your Spirit and they shall be created,

And you shall renew the face of the earth.

Fourth Mystery: The Holy Spirit in the church.

The Meditation: And suddenly from heaven there came a sound like the rush of a violent wind, and it filled the entire house where they were sitting.

All of them were filled with the Holy Spirit and began to speak in other languages, as the Spirit gave them ability.

 Cretans and Arabs—in our own languages we hear them speaking about mighty acts of God. (Acts 2: 2,4,11)

The Practice: Thank God for the privilege to be called his child and the child of the church. Uphold her doctrines, seek her interests and defend her rights.

Our Father

On the Small Beads: **Come Oh Holy Spirit and fill the heart of the faithful**....

Responds And enkindle in us the fire of your love. **(10 times)**

Send forth your Spirit and they shall be created,

And you shall renew the face of the earth.

Fifth Mystery: The Holy Spirit in the soul of the just man and just woman.

The Meditation:

(1)   Do you not know that your bodies are the temple of the Holy Spirit, who is in you? (1 Cor. 6:19.)

(2)   Extinguish not the Spirit. (1 Thess.5:19.)

(3)   And grieve not the Holy Spirit of God whereby you are sealed unto the day of redemption. (Eph.4: 30.)

The Practice: be ever mindful of the holy spirit who is within you, and carefully cultivate purity of soul and body. Faithfully obey his divine inspirations so that you may bring forth the fruits of the spirit — charity, joy, peace, patience, benignity, goodness, long-suffering, mildness, faith, modesty, continence, and chastity.

Our Father

On the Small Beads: **Come Oh Holy Spirit and fill the heart of the faithful**....

Responds And enkindle in us the fire of your love. **(10 times)**

Send forth your Spirit and they shall be created,

And you shall renew the face of the earth.

Let Us Pray

Father, pour out your spirit upon your faithful ones as you did on the Pentecost day and renew your signs and wonders in this our generation give us a new sight of your glory, a new encounter of your power, an obedient heart to your word and a new allegiance to be willing to serve you that your love may grow among us and your kingdom come through Christ our Lord...Amen.

Prayer to the Holy Spirit

O Holy Spirit, Spirit of Truth, of Love and of Holiness promised to us, coming from the Father and the Son and equal to Them in all things, I adore you and love you with all my heart. put in me the holy fear of God; give me the scruples and patience and do not permit me to fall into sin. increase in me Faith, Hope and Charity, and bring forth in my soul all the virtues proper to my state of life. Transform me to be a faithful disciple of Jesus Christ, and an obedient child of Holy Church. Give me the active grace to keep the Commandments and to receive the Sacraments worthily. May I possess the Four Cardinal Virtues, Thy Seven Gifts, Thy Twelve Fruits. Bring me up to perfection in the state of life to which you have called me; and lead me, through a happy death, to life everlasting through Jesus Christ Our Lord. Amen.

Aspirations to the Holy Spirit

LIGHT of the intellect, enlighten me;

Divine Fire of hearts, inflame me;

Fullness of souls, fill me;

Lord of grace and life, vivify me;

In this vale of suffering, guide me;

In my weakness, strengthen me;

From stumbles and falls, deliver me;

With Thy Divine Gifts, overwhelm me;

With Thy Presence, console me;

By Thy Divine operations, sanctify me;

Into my Jesus, transform me;

And unto Thy glory, bear me,

That, having been faithful upon earth,

I may enjoy eternal happiness in Heaven, wrapped within your perfect love.

Amen.

O eternal Love, I love you; please perfect and increase my love for you!

Dear HOLY SPIRIT, sweet Guest of my soul, dwell in me and grant that I may ever abide in your presence.

Prayer to the Holy Spirit for the Church

Great paraclete, be merciful to your holy Church; by your infinite power make her strong and secure against the attacks of her enemies and renew in her anointed servants the spirit of charity and grant them your efficacious , that they may glorify you and the Father and His only-begotten Son, Jesus Christ Our Lord. Amen.

Sighing for the Holy Spirit

O great Comforter, Holy Spirit, come to me. My soul yearns for you! My heart thirsts for you! you alone can satisfy my longing; you alone can make me happy. Do not reject, O Divine Bridegroom, the dwelling of my poor heart.

Behold My heart is not pure, but you can purify it.

My heart is filled with darkness, but you can illuminate it with your heavenly light.

My heart is filled with wickedness, but you can penetrate it with your divine love.

My heart is sad, but you can comfort it.

My heart is weak, but you can make it strong.

My heart is cold, but you can inflame it.

My heart clings to earthly things, but you can fill it with heavenly desires.

My heart is full of inequities, but you can adorn it with all virtues.

My heart is fickle and wayward, but you can make it docile.

Come dear, O Holy Spirit, you who is the Father of the poor, come and fill me with your love. Amen.

Father, Father, send us the promised Paraclete, through Jesus Christ Our Lord.

Prayer to Mary, Spouse of the Holy Spirit

O Mother MARY, you who was the spotless Bride of the Holy Spirit, you are the glory of Jerusalem, the joy of Israel, the honor of our people! you, as the Valiant Woman, did crushed the head of the ancient serpent when you offered up your Divine Son to the Heavenly Father, in the love of the Holy Spirit, for the salvation of the world. Through the merits of this precious Sacrifice and through the sufferings of your dearly beloved Son, obtain for us the Gifts of the Holy Spirit. I thank the Holy Spirit that He chose you as His Bride and made you the dispenser of His graces. Look upon me with your compassionate eyes; regard my distress and needs. Help me, that I may never lose the grace of God nor defile the temple of the Holy Spirit, but that my heart may ever remain His holy dwelling, and that with you I may praise and bless the Holy Spirit in Heaven forever and ever . Amen.

 Our Lady of Light, Spouse of the Holy Spirit, pray for us.

Prayer in Honor of the Holy Spirit

O Holy Spirit please reveal to me your personality, your presence, your power. Let me recognize your Sevenfold Gifts-----the Spirit of Wisdom and Understanding, of Counsel and

Fortitude, of Knowledge, Piety, and Fear of the Lord. O you Who is the Spirit of the Father and the Son, O you Who baptize with fire and infuse your love into our hearts-----please let one ray of that your holy light, one spark of that your holy fire inflame me and plunge me into the fire of Divine Love! Let this sacred fire flame up in me and destroy in me all that displeases you and which defiles my body or soul. Cleanse me in a sevenfold manner with your Gifts. Transform me into a holocaust, holy and acceptable to you. Inflame me with zeal so that I may live the life of grace and die the death of a repentant sinner, deeply penetrated by Thy Divine Love. Amen.

Act of Consecration to the Holy Spirit

O HOLY GHOST; Divine Spirit of light and love, I consecrate to Thee my understanding, my

heart and my will, my whole being, for time and eternity. May my understanding be always submissive to Thy heavenly inspirations and the teachings of the Catholic Church, of which you are the Infallible Guide. May my heart be ever inflamed with love of God and of my neighbor. May my will be ever conformed to the Divine will, and may my whole life be a faithful imitation of the life and virtues of our Lord and Savior Jesus Christ, to Whom, with

the Father and Thee, be honor and glory
forever. Amen.

Prayer for Sinners
O HOLY SPIRIT, Spirit of the Father and the
Son, let the strength of your love be ever more
felt in the hearts of men. Let Thy light shine
more and more on souls that are wandering in
the darkness far away from God. Turn them to
the light-giving Heart of Jesus and to the
healing stream of His Precious Blood.
Strengthen souls that love you. Perfect in them
your Seven Gifts and your Twelve Fruits, and
so make them your temples here on earth that
you may be adored in them forever. Amen.

Daily Consecration to the Holy Ghost

most holy Spirit receive the consecration that I
make of my entire being today to you . From
this moment on, come into every area of my
life and into each of my actions. you are my
Light, my Guide, my Strength, and the sole
desire of my heart. I abandon myself without
reserve to your Divine directions and action,
and I desire to be ever docile to your
inspirations. O Holy Ghost, transform me, with
and through Mary, into another Christ Jesus,
for the glory of the Father and the salvation of
the world. Amen.

Prayer for the Seven Gifts of the Holy Ghost

Dearest Jesus, Who before ascending into Heaven had promised to send the Holy Spirit to finish your work of redemption in the souls of your Apostles and Disciples, deign to grant the same Holy Spirit to me, that He may perfect in my soul the work of your grace and your love. Grant me the Spirit of Wisdom, that I may hold in contempt the passing things of this world and aspire only after the things that are eternal; the Spirit of Understanding, to enlighten my mind with the light of your Divine truth; the Spirit of Counsel, that I may ever choose the guaranteed way of pleasing God and gaining Heaven; the Spirit of Fortitude, that I may carry my cross with you and that I may overcome with courage all the obstacles that oppose my salvation; the Spirit of Knowledge, that I may know God and know myself and grow in perfection in the life of sainthood to which I am called; the Spirit of Piety, that I may find the service of God sweet and amiable; the Spirit of Fear, that I may be filled with a loving reverence towards God and may dread in any way to displease Him. Mark me, Dear Lord, with the sign of your true

disciples, and animate me in all things with
your Spirit. Amen.

Act of Oblation to the Holy Spirit

On My Knees before the great cloud of heavenly witnesses, I offer myself body and soul to Thee, eternal Spirit of God. I adore the brightness of your purity, the unerring keenness of your justice and the might of Thy love. You are the strength and light of my soul. In you I live and move and have my being. I desire never to grieve you through sin, and I pray with all my heart to be kept safe from the smallest sin against you. Grant that I may be faithful in every thought, words and deeds, and grant that I may always listen to your voice, watch for your light, and follow your gracious inspirations. I cling to you and give myself to you, and I ask you by your compassion to watch over me in my weakness. Holding the pierced feet of Jesus, looking at His five Wounds, trusting in His Precious Blood and adoring His sacred side and stricken Heart, I implore Thee, adorable Spirit, Helper of my infirmity, to keep me in your grace that I may never sin against you with the sin which you will not forgive. Grant to me the grace, O Holy Spirit, Spirit of the Father and of the Son, to say to you always and everywhere, "Speak, Lord, for your servant hears." Amen.

Prayer for Unity

Dear Holy Spirit, Spirit of Truth, come into our hearts; shed the brightness of your light upon the nations, that they may please you in unity of faith.

Hymn to the Holy Spirit

O COME, Creator Spirit, come;
        The souls which are Thine own invade;
And with supernal grace inflame
The hearts which Thou Thyself hast made.

O Thou Who art the Comforter,
The Gift of God most high,
The living fount of fire and love,
Celestial unction from above.

O Thou Who art of sevenfold power,
The finger of the Father's hand,
The fullness of His promised Word,
Who hast all speech at Thy command.

Enkindle light within our minds,
With love our wayward hearts inflame;
And with Thine own undying life,
Give vigor to our mortal frame.

Drive far from us the angry foe,
And Thy true peace impart within,
That, Thou our Leader and our Guide,

We may escape the snares of sin.

Through Thee may we the Father know,

Through Thee approach the Eternal Son,

And Thee, the Spirit of Them both,

Confess while endless ages run.

To God the Father glory be,

And to the Son from death arisen,

And to the blessed Paraclete,

Be praise and ceaseless honor given. Amen.

Sequence of Pentecost

O HOLY SPIRIT! Lord of light!
 From Thy clear celestial height
Thy pure and beaming radiance give.

Come, Thou Father of the poor!
Come, with treasures which endure!
Come, Thou light of all that live!

Thou of all Consolers best,
Visiting the troubled breast,
 Dost refreshing peace bestow.

Thou in toil art Comfort sweet,
Pleasant coolness in the heat,
Solace in the midst of woe.

Light immortal! Light Divine!
Visit Thou these hearts of Thine,
And our inmost being fill.

If Thou take Thy grace away,

Nothing pure in man will stay;

All his good is turned to ill.

Heal our wounds, our strength renew;

On our dryness, pour Thy dew;

Wash the stains of guilt away.

Bend the stubborn heart and will;

Melt the frozen, warm the chill;

Guide the steps that go astray.

Thou, on those who evermore

Thee confess and Thee adore,

In Thy sevenfold Gifts descend.

Give them comfort when they die;

Give them life with Thee on high;

Give them joys which never end. Amen.